P9-CLE-181

What To Do About Alice?

How
ALICE ROOSEVELT
broke
THE RULES,
charmed
THE WORLD,
and drove her
FATHER TEDDY
CRAZY!

LIBRARY
FRANKLIN PIERCE UNIVERSITY
RINDGE, NH 03461

by
BARBARA KERLEY

Illustrated by
EDWIN FOTHERINGHAM

SCHOLASTIC PRESS   NEW YORK

Theodore Roosevelt had a small problem.

CURR
E
757.3
.R47
2008

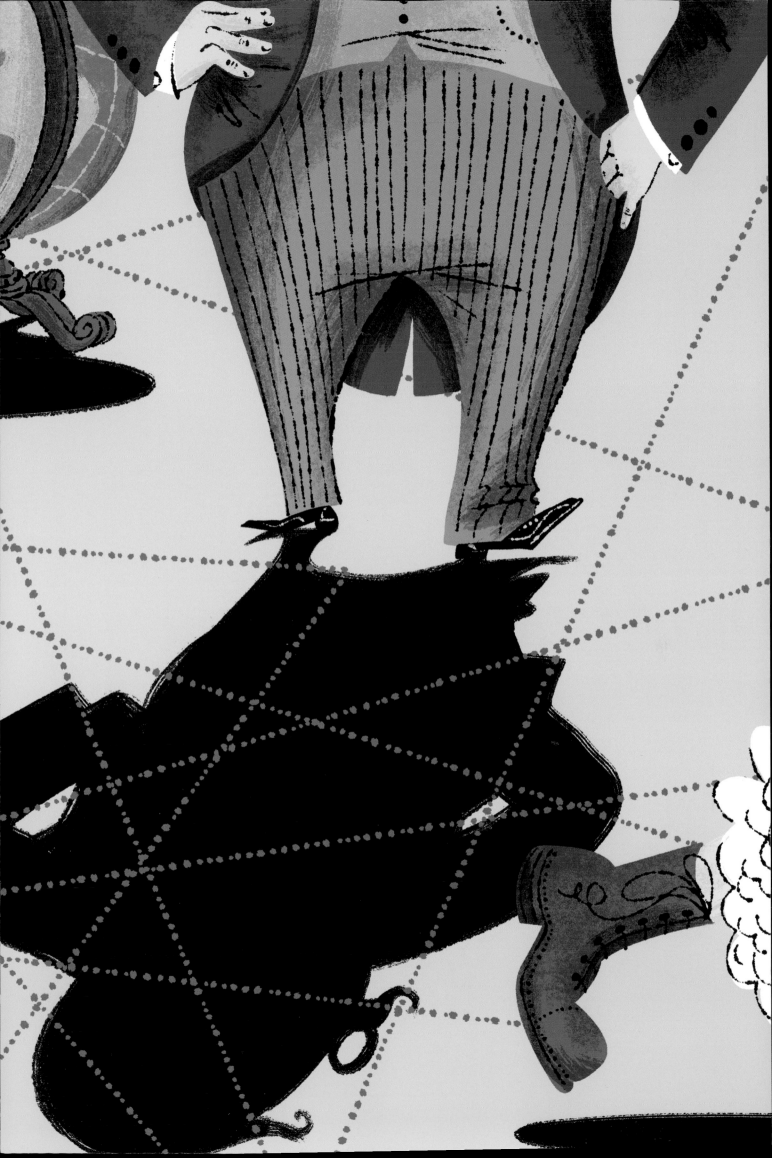

It wasn't herding thousands of cattle across the Dakota badlands.
HE'D DONE THAT.

It wasn't leading

the Rough Riders as they

charged up Kettle Hill.

HE'D

DONE

THAT,

TOO.

He'd bagged a grizzly bear,
captured outlaws, governed the state
of New York, and served as vice president
of the United States, and *still*
he had a problem.

Her name was Alice.
Alice Lee Roosevelt
was hungry to *go*
places, *meet*
people, *do*
things.

Father called it **"RUNNING RIOT."**

Alice called it *"eating up the world."*

From the time she was a little girl,

Alice ate up the world.

Her mother had died in 1884, two days after Alice was born. Father was sad.

Everyone was sad for Alice. But she didn't remember her mother. She did not want

to grow up hearing them say, **"THE POOR LITTLE THING!"**

She wanted to see how high the springs sprang on her grandparents' favorite sofa.

Father remarried and had more children. But every morning Alice still cried, **"NOW, PIG!"** until Father gave her a piggyback ride downstairs to breakfast.

The family moved between New York and Washington, D.C., following

Father's jobs. Wherever they went, Alice ate up the world.

She rowed across Oyster Bay for picnics on the beach.

She gamboled through the parks of Washington

pretending to be a fiery horse.

She learned to love crusty French rolls

and English tea served "piping hot."

She read voraciously and drank

in Father's tales of Davy Crockett,

George Armstrong Custer,

and Daniel Boone.

Instead of going to school, Alice was taught at home,
with lots of time for exploring. In New York City,
she watched the students of Miss Spence's boarding
school walk oh-so-primly down the sidewalk.
That didn't look like much fun to Alice.
She wanted to own a pet monkey and wear pants.

As Alice got older, doctors noticed

that her legs weren't growing properly.

For the next several years, she'd have

to wear braces.

Sometimes while she walked or ran,

the braces would lock up, pitching

Alice face-first to the ground.

She did not want anyone saying

"THE POOR LITTLE THING!"

about *that*, either.

When Alice's leg braces finally came off, Father encouraged her to ride a bicycle. He hoped it would help her feel less **"CAUTIOUS."**

Alice loved her new freedom. She roamed the streets of Washington

from the Capitol steps to the gypsy camps by the racetrack.

She joined an all-boys club.

The boys arrived in disguise . . .

until Father discovered the ruse.

He grumbled. Alice was

"UNRULY" and **"INCONSIDERATE."**

She was turning into

a **TOMBOY!**

ENOUGH WAS ENOUGH: It was time for *Alice* to

attend Miss Spence's boarding school and learn to be a proper

young lady.

Alice was appalled. The idea completely **"SHRIVELED"** her.

Every afternoon, all summer long, she made a point of going

to her room to weep.

Father couldn't bear to see Alice so unhappy.

When school started in the fall, Alice stayed home after all.

She came up with her own solution for her education.

She said to Father, **"LET ME LOOSE IN YOUR LIBRARY."**

She taught herself astronomy, geology, even Greek grammar.

She read Twain, Dickens, Darwin, and the Bible, cover to cover.

Every morning she told Father what she had learned the day before.

She also grew ever more curious about politics as Father's career soared

higher and higher: the discussions around the breakfast table, the stream

of people seeking Father's advice, and the excitement of election night.

In 1901, when Alice was seventeen, Father became president of the

United States. The whole family moved into the White House.

Alice tried to be helpful. She watched her younger brothers and

sister so her stepmother could get some rest.

With her pet snake, Emily Spinach—which Alice had named for its
color and its resemblance to a very thin aunt—she welcomed Father's visitors.
He sputtered to a friend, "I can be president of the United States, or I can
control Alice. I cannot possibly **DO BOTH.**"

As daughter of the president,
Alice assumed her role as
goodwill ambassador.

She helped open the Buffalo Exposition,
riding a camel and watching the hoochee-
koochee dancers.

She christened the kaiser's yacht with great fanfare
and a large bottle of champagne.

She visited plantations in Cuba and schools in Puerto Rico,
all on her **"BEST OFFICIAL BEHAVIOR."**

Father delightedly wrote to her: "You were of real service down
there because you made those people feel that you liked them and
took an interest in them, and your presence was accepted as
a great compliment. . . ."

He warned Alice time and again, however, not to let
newspaper reporters catch her gallivanting around.

He reminded her that **"NICE"** people did not want
to see their names in the paper.

"BEWARE OF PUBLICITY!" Father said.

"DO NOT TALK TO REPORTERS!"

MISS ROOSEVELT MISSED FROM PEW.

Did Not Attend Church Yesterday.

...ing Stares
...rious

SOCIETY GOSSIP FROM WASHIN...

MISS RO... SAVES A D...

Casino Manager Rescued Dances...
Languishing to Deat...

BAD ...EA...

EVERYONE LOVED ALICE. A songwriter wrote "Alice, Where Art Thou?"

and bands everywhere played it. Mothers named their baby girls "Alice."

Alice even had a color named after her—Alice Blue—

that matched the color of her blue-gray eyes.

The press called her "Princess Alice."

Other young ladies rode in carriages. Alice drove her runabout. *Fast.*

She two-stepped till the wee hours of the morning.

She was even caught betting on a horse race.

Letters poured in to Father from conservative women's groups.

Alice's behavior was **OUTRAGEOUS**, they said.

In 1905, Father began his second term as president. As he was being sworn in,

Alice waved madly to her friends until Father finally told her to **SIT DOWN.**

"You're making a show of yourself," he grumbled.

"Well, you do it," Alice protested. "Why shouldn't I?"

"But this is my inauguration!" Father replied.

He got right back to work, brokering a peace treaty between Russia and Japan. Meanwhile, Alice asked if she might join the American delegation heading to Asia. The papers trumpeted the news:

EXTRA

ALICE IN WONDERLAND

How First Maiden of Land Will Travel to Orient

TO CROSS PACIFIC IN FLOATING PALACE—
WILL HAVE HER OWN SUITE OF ROOMS ABOARD...
WHAT SHE WILL SEE IN THE WONDERLANDS
ACROSS THE PACIFIC...
TROPICAL ROMANCE ANTICIPATED

Alice boarded

the ship in San Francisco

with two large hatboxes, four

trunks, and oodles of boxes and bags.

Alice had a marvelous time. She danced the hula in Hawaii.

She jumped fully clothed into the ship's swimming pool. She

watched sumo wrestling in Japan, reviewed the troops in the

Philippines, and toured the gardens of the empress of China,

receiving many gifts along the way.

After four months, Alice returned with two large hatboxes,

four trunks, oodles of boxes and bags, and twenty-three cases

of **"LOOT."**

Father

was not

amused.

Alice also brought home a fiancé,

Nicholas Longworth, a debonair congressman who had

been on the trip. And what did she want for wedding presents?

"**TRINKETS,**" said Alice. "Preferably *diamond* trinkets."

From all over the world, friends, dignitaries, and total strangers

sent her gifts: jewelry, fur coats, silver vases, cakes, clocks, furniture,

sewing machines, washing machines, popcorn, bales of hay,

a load of coal, a box of snakes, a pair of turtledoves, and a Boston terrier

with its own wardrobe of dog clothes. She even got a pet monkey.

"She'll accept

anything,"

friends said,

"except a red-hot stove!"

The White House wedding was the social event of the season.

Eight hundred guests watched Father walk Alice down the aisle.

Alice jumped into her new role as wife of a congressman, hurrying home from
Congress for quick meals of scrambled eggs before rushing back to hear the debates.
But she was still the daughter of the president. As her love and knowledge of politics
grew, she quickly became one of Father's most trusted advisers and ardent champions.

And she still ate up the world,
dancing the turkey trot at diplomatic balls
and playing poker with the boys.
She even created the Night Riders,
who galloped to the houses of
friends and bellowed
until invited in for snacks.

And Father?

Even after he left the presidency,

he remained one of the country's most popular politicians, leading

Americans in times of hardship and prosperity.

But there was one problem

that Theodore Roosevelt

never quite solved . . .

What to do about Alice?

Author's Note

"SISTER"

THEODORE ROOSEVELT deeply loved his first wife, Alice Lee. He called her his "sunny darling" and wrote in his diary, "If loving her with my whole heart and soul can make her happy, she shall be happy."

He was equally grief-stricken when she died, stating, "The light has gone out of my life."

Baby Alice grew up with a photograph of her mother on the wall above her bed. Her nanny instructed, "Say a prayer for your little mother in heaven."

Yet Theodore never spoke of his first wife again. "He never even said her name," Alice later remembered. In fact, he sometimes even avoided calling his daughter "Alice," often referring to her as "Sister" with his other children.

Growing up, Alice never quite felt like she "belonged" in the family the way her stepsiblings did. Some historians speculate that Alice spent her time gallivanting around in part because she never felt completely comfortable at home.

"PRINCESS ALICE"

IN JANUARY 1903, Theodore Roosevelt complained to his son about nineteen-year-old "Alice, who generally only makes her appearance well after noon, having been up until all hours dancing the night before." He worried that Alice's "life of social excitement" was not healthy for a young lady.

It was also potentially embarrassing for the whole family. Alice's very public high jinks—zooming around town in her car, dancing all night, betting on horse races—shocked people who felt that young ladies should behave with more restraint. A newspaper once even reported—incorrectly, Alice later claimed—that she had been seen at a fancy party dancing on the roof in her underwear.

Alice was certainly ahead of her time. But for all the people who felt that Alice had gone too far, many more were captivated by her zest for fun. They eagerly scanned the papers for the latest news about her. In an era before movie stars, "Princess Alice" was a celebrity with many adoring fans.

Historians generally agree that Alice's celebrity status bolstered Theodore's own popularity, and that he appreciated this help. They also say that Alice was probably Theodore's favorite of all his six children.

After Alice's 1903 goodwill tour of Puerto Rico, he wrote to her:

> *Darling Alice: I was really delighted with your letter, and before I received it I had been very much pleased with all I had heard of how you had acted in Porto Rico. I am very much pleased that you found the visit so interesting; and it was a good thing in more ways than one. You were of real service down there because you made those people feel that you liked them and took an interest in them, and your presence was accepted as a great compliment. . . .*
>
> *Goodbye blessed girl. . . .*
>
> *Your loving father*